BIBLE
Activity Book

Suzanne Ross

DOVER PUBLICATIONS, INC.
Mineola, New York

Bibliographical Note

Bible Activity Book is a new work, first published by Dover Publications, Inc., in 2002.

International Standard Book Number: 0-486-42335-2

Manufactured in the United States of America
Dover Publications, Inc., 31 East 2nd Street, Mineola, N.Y. 11501

NOTE

In this book you will find activities such as mazes, crossword puzzles, and connect-the-dots—all based on stories from the Old Testament Bible. You will read about Jacob's ladder, Noah's ark, and the whale that swallowed Jonah, among many other favorite stories. Solutions begin on page 53, but don't peek until you've done all of the puzzles yourself! You can also have fun coloring every page as well. Enjoy!

Find the path that will take baby Moses in his basket to
Pharaoh's daughter. [Exodus 2:6]

5

Connect the dots to see the animal that would not take
Balaam the Magician to harm the Israelites. [Numbers 22:21]

Help Ruth pick up all four bundles of grain as she walks
along the path to reach Naomi. [Ruth 2:18]

7

Color this picture of Queen Esther telling the King of
Persia of the plot against her people. [Esther 7:6]

8

Jacob is dreaming about a ladder that reaches to heaven.
Find the path that leads to the ladder. [Genesis 28:12]

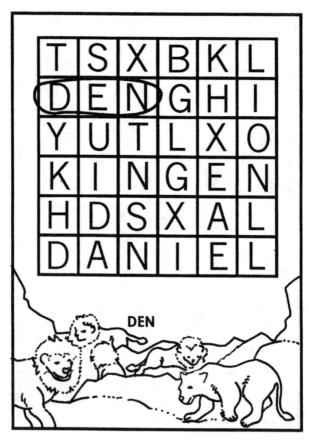

T	S	X	B	K	L
D	E	N	G	H	I
Y	U	T	L	X	O
K	I	N	G	E	N
H	D	S	X	A	L
D	A	N	I	E	L

DEN

Daniel was thrown into the lion's den by order of
King Darius. [Daniel 6:16]

KING

DANIEL

LION

Find and circle in the puzzle on the facing page
the three words from the story. Example: DEN.

The king was quite surprised to find that Daniel was still alive! Follow the path from the king to Daniel. [Daniel 6:22]

12

Gabriel was sent to Daniel to explain to him some events
that were to take place in the future. Connect the dots to
see a picture of Gabriel. [Daniel 8:15–16]

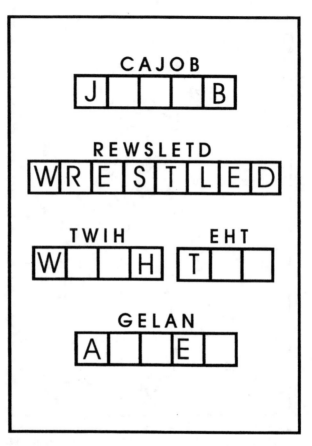

CAJOB

| J | | | | B |

REWSLETD

| W | R | E | S | T | L | E | D |

TWIH

| W | | | H |

EHT

| T | | |

GELAN

| A | | E | |

The picture on the facing page shows a fierce struggle
from a famous Bible story. [Genesis 32:24]

To tell about the picture, unscramble the letters above the boxes to spell out the words. Example: WRESTLED.

Moses received the Ten Commandments from God.
These rules told people the proper way to live their lives.
Color this picture of Moses. [Exodus 31:18]

The people of Moses had to stop worshiping the golden calf and begin to worship God. Color this picture of the worship of the golden calf. [Exodus 32:8]

17

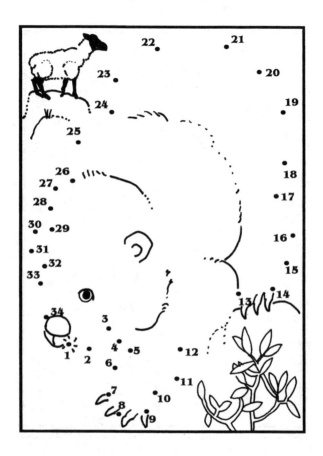

David took care of his father's sheep. Connect the dots to see what animal tried to harm the sheep. [1 Samuel 17:34]

18

Connect the black stars to find out what Abraham is learning about his future. [Genesis 17:16]

19

Noah built an ark to save his family from the coming flood that would destroy everything. He also gathered two or more of each kind of animal. [Genesis 7:2]

20

Use the picture clues to complete
the crossword puzzle.

Here is a picture of the animals making their way to Noah's ark. Look carefully. Find and circle the three things that are wrong in the picture. [Genesis 7:8–9]

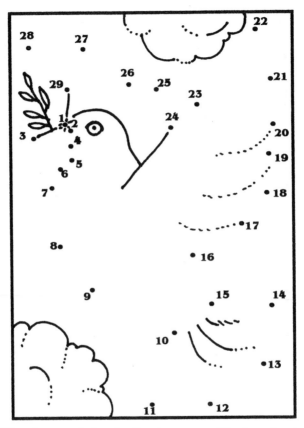

When it seemed that the flood was over, Noah sent out one of the animals from the ark to find land. Connect the dots to see a picture of this animal. [Genesis 8:8]

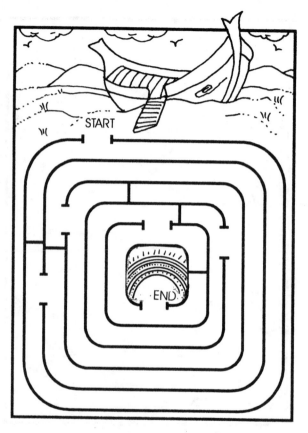

START

END

After the flood, a beautiful rainbow appeared in the sky.
Find the path that leads from the ark to
the rainbow. [Genesis 9:13]

24

Joseph's brothers want to ask the governor of Egypt for corn. Help them find the path that leads to the governor. [Genesis 42:1–3]

Samson's great strength came from his long hair. His
enemies had Delilah cut it short. When it grew back, he
pulled down the temple pillars. Find the path that
leads to Samson. [Judges 16:17; 16:29–30]

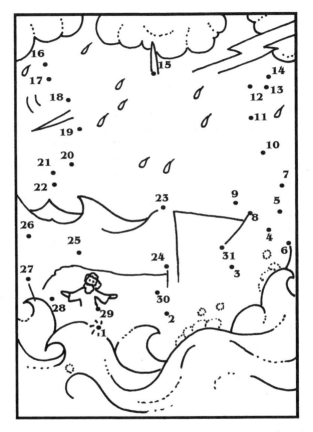

God asked Jonah to go on a mission, but Jonah refused.
He decided to run away. Suddenly, a violent storm began.
Connect the dots to see how Jonah escaped. [Jonah 1:1–4]

27

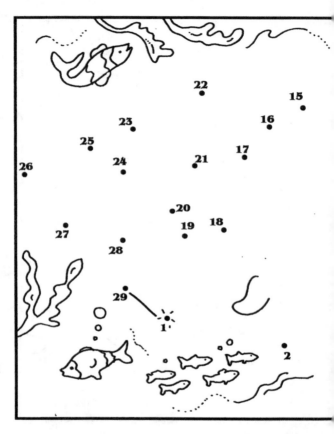

The sailors thought that Jonah was to blame for the storm, so they threw him overboard. They hoped that this would put an end to the storm. [Jonah 1:10–15]

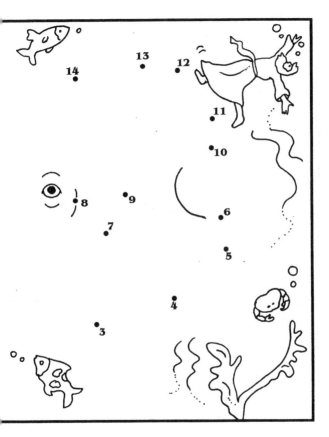

But Jonah was about to have even bigger problems.
Connect the dots to see what God had prepared for
Jonah in the sea. [Jonah 1:17]

Goliath was twice as tall as David, but David was able to knock Goliath down with a stone. Find and color three soldiers who are hidden in this picture. [1 Samuel 17:49–50]

Each picture on one side goes with a picture on the other side. Draw a line connecting the two. Example: Baby Moses and the basket.

Here is a picture of something very famous that you can read about in a Bible story. [Genesis 37:3]

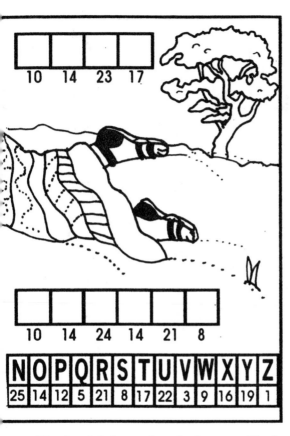

10	14	23	17

10	14	24	14	21	8

N	O	P	Q	R	S	T	U	V	W	X	Y	Z
25	14	12	5	21	8	17	22	3	9	16	19	1

Use the alphabet code at the bottom of both
pages to spell out the words in the puzzle. A
letter in one of the words has been done.

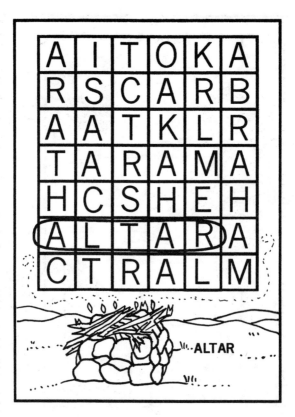

As a test, God asked Abraham to sacrifice his son Isaac.
Abraham was ready to do this. But God gave him a lamb
in place of his son. Abraham had passed the test.
[Genesis 22:2; 22:8–13]

ABRAHAM

ISAAC

RAM

Find and circle each word from the story in the puzzle on the facing page. Example: ALTAR.

The desert lands of the Bible are hot and dry. Here is a
picture of a boy and his camels. Find three things that do
not belong in this picture and circle them.

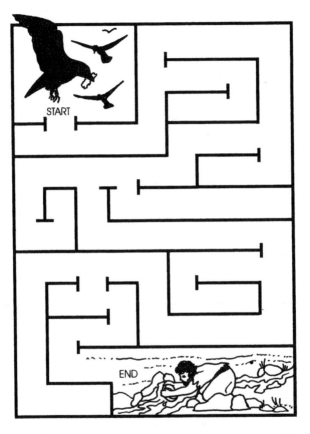

START

END

God was angry and dried up the land. But He sent thirsty
Elijah to a stream and sent ravens with food. Help the
ravens find Elijah. [1 Kings 17:3–6]

Gideon destroyed a statue of a false god. He then made a
plan to destroy the enemy. Help Gideon find the path to
the broken pitcher that he used to frighten an enemy
soldier. [Judges 6:25–28; 7: 19–20]

Joshua sent two spies to Jericho. Rahab risked her life by hiding the spies from the king's men. Find and color in the two spies and a soldier. [Joshua 2:1–6]

39

Each picture on one side goes with a picture on the other side. Draw a line connecting the two.
Example: David and Goliath.

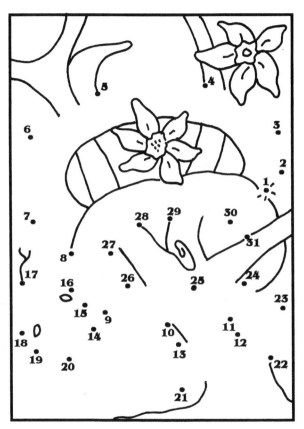

This animal persuaded Eve to eat the fruit that had been
forbidden to her and Adam in the Garden of Eden.
Connect the dots to see this animal. [Genesis 3:1–6]

41

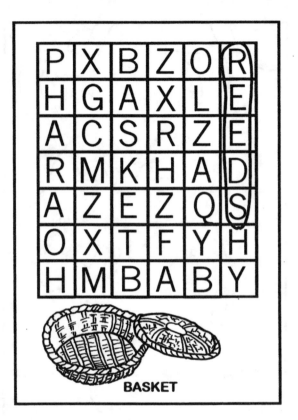

BASKET

Pharaoh ordered that the male babies of the Israelites be
killed. A baby boy was put on the river in a basket and
saved. This baby was Moses, who became the leader of
his people. [Exodus 1:16; 2:3]

42

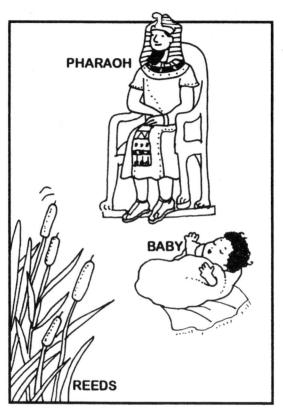

Pharaoh's daughter found the baby Moses in the reeds by
the river. Here are some pictures from this story. Find and
circle each word in the puzzle. Example: REEDS.
[Exodus 2:5]

43

START

END

Deborah wants to free her people by defeating Sisera and
his army. Help Deborah find the path to Mount
Tabor to fight the enemy. [Judges 4:6–7]

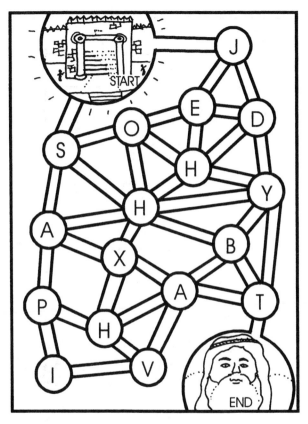

One of the kings who ruled in Abraham's temple was
Jehoshaphat. Draw a line connecting each letter of his
name—without touching any other letters—
to reach him. [2 Chronicles 17–20]

To get to the promised land, the Israelites had to capture the city of Jericho. God told Joshua, the leader of the Israelites, how to succeed. After a week, the Israelites took over Jericho. [Joshua 1–6]

46

Here are some pictures about the story of the battle of Jericho. Use these picture clues to complete the puzzle.

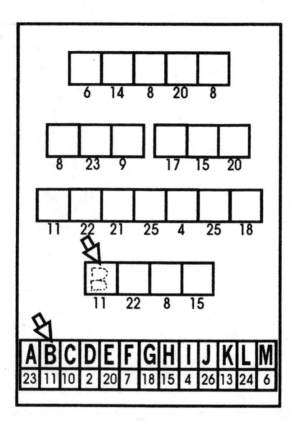

Moses was tending his sheep when he saw a strange sight:
a bush was in flames but was not burning itself out! He
was even more surprised when he heard the voice of God.
[Exodus 3]

48

N	O	P	Q	R	S	T	U	V	W	X	Y	Z
25	14	12	5	21	8	17	22	3	9	16	19	1

Use the alphabet code at the bottom of both pages to
spell out the words in the puzzle. A letter in one
of the words has been done for you.

K	F	T	X	L	S
S	A	E	O	E	N
C	D	V	I	L	A
L	A	E	E	X	K
A	M	U	L	L	E
G	A	R	D	E	N

GARDEN

For a while, Adam and Eve lived happy, peaceful lives in
the Garden of Eden. Then the spiteful snake
changed their lives forever. [Genesis 3]

Here are some pictures from the story of Adam and Eve.
Find and circle each word in the puzzle.
Example: GARDEN.

Color this picture of Moses. He has just parted the Red
Sea so that his people could escape to freedom.
[Exodus 14:21–22]

SOLUTIONS

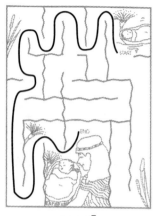

page 5

page 6

page 7

page 9

page 10

page 12

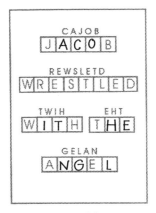

page 13

CAJOB
J A C O B

REWSLETD
W R E S T L E D

TWIH   EHT
W I T H   T H E

GELAN
A N G E L

page 14

55

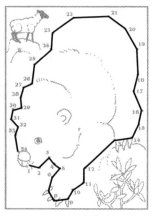

page 18

page 19

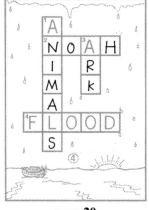

page 20

page 22

56

page 23

page 24

page 25

page 26

page 27

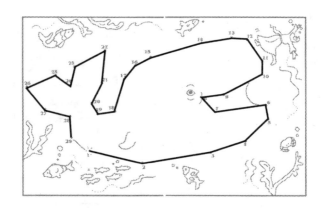

page 28   **page 29**

page 30

page 31

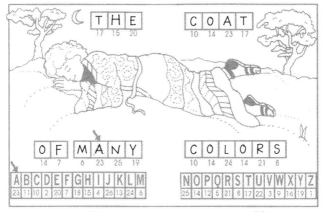

page 32   **page 33**

page 34

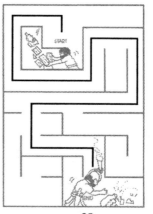

page 36

page 37

page 38

60

page 39

page 40

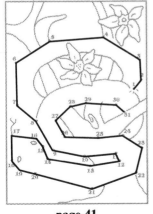

page 41

P	X	B	Z	O	R
H	G	A	X	L	E
A	C	S	R	Z	E
R	M	K	H	A	D
A	Z	E	Z	Q	S
O	X	T	F	Y	H
H	M	B	A	B	Y

BASKET

page 42

61

page 44

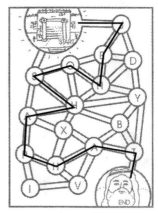

page 45

page 46

62

page 48

page 50

63